TARANTULAS

by Vicky Franchino

Children's Press®

An Imprint of Scholastic Inc.
New York   Toronto   London   Auckland   Sydney
Mexico City   New Delhi   Hong Kong
Danbury, Connecticut

Content Consultant
Dr. Stephen S. Ditchkoff
Professor of Wildlife Sciences
Auburn University
Auburn, Alabama

Photographs © 2012: age fotostock/ARCO/P.Wegner: 11; AP
Images: 40 (George Nikitin), 39 (Vincent Thian); Bob Italiano: 44
foreground, 45 foreground; Dreamstime: cover (Cathy Keifer), 2
background, 3 (Dorothy Kye), 44 background, 45 background
(Piotr Sikora); iStockphoto/Marcelo Casacuberta: 5 bottom,
36; Minden Pictures/Konrad Wothe: 15; Photo Researchers: 27
(Francesco Tomasinelli), 28 (Louise K. Broman); Shutterstock, Inc.: 20
(Audrey Snider-Bell), 30, 31 (Cathy Keifer), 32 (EcoPrint), 5 top, 8
(worldswildlifewonders); Superstock: 19 (imagebroker.net), 1, 2 inset,
4, 5 background, 7, 12, 16, 23, 24 (Minden Pictures); US Fish &
Wildlife Service: 35.

Library of Congress Cataloging-in-Publication Data
Franchino, Vicky.
  Tarantulas/by Vicky Franchino.
      p. cm.—(Nature's children)
  Includes bibliographical references and index.
  ISBN-13: 978-0-531-20908-0 (lib. bdg.)
      ISBN-10: 0-531-20908-3 (lib. bdg.)
  ISBN-13: 978-0-531-21083-3 (pbk.)
      ISBN-10: 0-531-21083-9 (pbk.)
  1. Tarantulas—Juvenile literature. I. Title. II. Series.
  QL458.42.T5F73 2012
  595.4'4—dc23   2011031085

All rights reserved. Published in 2012 by Children's Press, an imprint
of Scholastic Inc.
Printed in China 62
SCHOLASTIC, CHILDREN'S PRESS, and associated logos are
trademarks and/or registered trademarks of Scholastic Inc.

1 2 3 4 5 6 7 8 9 10 R 21 20 19 18 17 16 15 14 13 12

Tarantulas

Class	Arachnida
Order	Araneae
Family	Theraposidae
Genus	More than 100 genera
Species	About 900 species
World distribution	Warm climates around the world including Africa, South and Central America, Asia, India, Australia and the United States
Habitats	Deserts, tropical rain forests, and other warm habitats
Distinctive physical characteristics	Most range in color from tan to reddish-brown to black and blend into their surroundings; have eight legs and two "mini legs" called pedipalps; are covered with barbed hairs that can be used as a weapon; have an exoskeleton that is shed throughout life; legs can be up to 4 inches (10 centimeters) long; teeth are hinged at the jaws like fangs
Habits	Active mostly at night; some wait for food to come to them, and others actively hunt; uses vibration to sense the approach of another animal; liquefies food before eating it
Diet	Insects, mice, snakes, lizards, birds, frogs, toads, and other spiders

TARANTULAS

Contents

CHAPTER 1

The World of Tarantulas

People often use words such as *hairy*, *scary*, and *big* to describe tarantulas. Tarantulas can be huge and frightful looking. But they're actually quite harmless and shy. A tarantula would probably run away if you saw one in the wild!

Tarantulas live in many different places around the world. You can find them in rain forests, deserts, and other warm climates. They don't care if the weather is wet or dry.

Scientists have discovered about 900 different types of tarantulas. Some are tiny, and some are gigantic! The biggest spider on Earth is called the Goliath bird-eating tarantula. Its leg span can be up to 12 inches (30 centimeters) wide. Would you be scared to have a spider the size of a dinner plate walking toward you?

Adult male
6 ft. (1.8 m)

Tarantula
12 in. (30 cm)

Even the huge Goliath bird-eating tarantula is not very dangerous to most people.

Spiders and Insects

Tarantulas might seem like insects, but they're not. They are actually spiders. Insects and spiders are different from each other in some important ways. Insects have six legs and antennae. Some have wings. Spiders have eight legs and no antennae or wings. Insects have a three-part body. Spiders' bodies have two parts.

Spiders and insects do have some things in common, though. Both have jointed legs. Both are invertebrates. This means they do not have backbones. Instead, they have hard outer skeletons called exoskeletons. Vertebrates are creatures with backbones. You are a vertebrate!

The front part of a tarantula's body is called the cephalothorax. This is where you'll find the tarantula's brain, eyes, jaws, and stomach. The cephalothorax is also home to four pairs of legs and a set of pedipalps. The pedipalps are small arms that the tarantula can use for many different jobs. They are covered with sensitive hairs that the tarantula uses to tell if something is safe to eat.

Some tarantulas have interesting color patterns.

Dinner Time

Tarantulas are **carnivores**. They eat animals such as insects and mice. Some can even eat a snake or a small bird. Tarantulas do not have teeth to chew their food. This means they have to digest their food before eating. A tarantula dribbles a special liquid on its **prey** after paralyzing it. This liquid makes the inside of the tarantula's meal turn gooey. Then the tarantula uses its stomach muscles like a giant straw to suck up its meal.

The tarantula's jaws are called **chelicerae**. They end in sharp fangs that the tarantula uses to stab its prey. Poisonous **venom paralyzes** the prey when the tarantula bites down.

Some tarantulas wait for their food to come to them. Others go out and hunt. They usually do their hunting at night. This makes it easier for the tarantula to hide. It also keeps the tarantula from becoming dinner for one of its **predators**!

Tarantulas grip captured prey in their chelicerae.

Blood and Breath

A tarantula's heart and simple **circulatory system** are found in the rear section of the body. This body section is known as the abdomen. In the human body, blood travels to and from the heart in tubes called arteries and veins. But in tarantulas, blood comes out of the heart and pours around the inside of its body. It then returns to the heart through **valves**.

It is very easy for a tarantula to lose a lot of blood if it is injured and starts to bleed. This can be a big problem. The tarantula uses the force of blood pumping through its body to move its legs. It won't be able to move if it loses too much blood or doesn't drink enough water.

The tarantula also has two sets of book lungs in its abdomen. They are called book lungs because they are made up of delicate sheets of tissue that look like the pages of a book.

Tarantulas get most of their water from their food, but they also need to drink sometimes.

Silk Spinning

The tarantula's silk **glands** are at the base of the abdomen. The silk leaves the tarantula's body as a liquid thread through tiny channels known as **spinnerets**. The tarantula pulls the thread out of the spinnerets with its legs. The thread becomes hard and very strong as it leaves the spider's body. Spider silk is five times as tough as a steel thread of the same width.

Some spiders make webs out of their silk. Tarantulas do not. Tarantulas use silk to make their homes, protect their eggs, or build **trip lines**. These threads of silk are attached to the tarantula's nest. The trip line starts to move when prey bumps it. Then the tarantula knows it's almost time for dinner!

An area called the **pedicle** lies between the cephalothorax and the abdomen. This is the tarantula's waist. The pedicle allows the tarantula to bend its body.

Many tarantulas build their nests on the ground.

Surviving in a Tough World

Tarantulas have to protect themselves from many different enemies. Their predators include weasels, coyotes, skunks, snakes, and birds.

Hairs on a tarantula's legs and pedipalps allow it to travel along many different types of surfaces. The spider uses these hairs to smell, taste, hear, and see, as well. Tarantulas also have claws on the ends of their legs. They use the claws to climb trees, walls, and other surfaces.

Most tarantulas have eight eyes. But their vision isn't very good. Their eyes can only tell the difference between light and dark, and can detect if something is moving nearby. They make up for this poor vision by using their hairs to feel **vibrations** that occur when another creature is close by.

Tarantulas cannot notice other creatures unless they are fairly close by.

Defending Against Predators

The tarantula has some excellent ways to defend itself. Its first survival skill is to make itself look big and scary. The tarantula will rear up on its back legs to appear as large and frightening as possible. Sometimes this is enough to scare off an attacker.

One of the most unusual ways that a tarantula protects itself is by being able to regrow its legs. The spider can break off its leg and escape if a predator attacks. The leg will grow back later.

A tarantula is covered with short, **barbed** hairs. Some tarantulas use their legs to rub the hairs off and flick them at enemies. Others simply rub their bodies on their attackers. Sometimes tarantulas pull out so many hairs that they get bald spots!

 **FUN FACT!** The pepsis wasp lays its eggs inside of living tarantulas. When the eggs hatch, they eat the tarantula from the inside out.

It is common for many animals to make themselves look larger in order to scare off enemies.

Tarantula Armor

The tarantula's body has a hard, protective covering made of **chitin**. It is thinner in spots where the tarantula needs to bend and thicker in places that need extra protection. The section over the tarantula's head is especially thick. It is called the **carapace**.

One time when tarantulas can't protect themselves is when they are **molting**. Their hard exoskeletons can't grow with them, so they have to shed them. A tarantula can't move or escape while waiting for a new exoskeleton to form and harden. The tarantula is in big trouble if an enemy finds him! Males stop molting once they're fully grown. Females continue to grow and to molt throughout their lives.

Tarantulas are usually good at protecting themselves. They live longer than other spiders. Scientists believe that male tarantulas can live up to six years in the wild. There have been female tarantulas that lived as long as 35 years!

Tarantulas leave behind empty exoskeletons when they molt.

Home Sweet Home

The tarantula's home is designed with safety in mind. Some tarantulas live in burrows. A tarantula digs its burrow deep into the ground using its jaws and pedipalps. The burrow is not much wider than the spider is. The opening is usually quite narrow. This keeps insects and other animals from getting into it. The tarantula lines the burrow with silk. This strong netting keeps the walls from collapsing around the spider.

A tarantula will often close up the entrance to the burrow with silk and stay inside during the winter. Tarantulas don't like cold weather. They can go without food for weeks.

Not all tarantulas live in burrows. Some live in logs or caves. Others live in crops such as bananas or pineapples or on trees. Those that live on trees or plants spin themselves silk tubes for shelter.

Tarantulas often build their burrows in dirt or sand.

CHAPTER 3

A Tarantula's Life Cycle

Tarantulas like to be alone. They live alone. They hunt alone. They eat alone. But one time when they have to be in contact with other tarantulas is when they **mate**.

Most types of tarantulas mate during a specific time of year. This is usually when the weather is hot and dry. The male tarantula goes in search of a female during mating season. But he must be very careful. Males are smaller than females. Females are often **cannibals**. The male taps a special sound on the ground. This lets the female know he is interested in mating, not in becoming dinner!

The female tarantula usually lays 500 to 1,000 eggs at a time. The mother spider wraps the eggs in silk and creates an **egg sac** to protect them until they're ready to hatch. This sac is sometimes nearly as big as she is! The tarantula puts the sac in a safe place until the babies are born.

Males sometimes catch the attention of potential mates by tearing at the entrances of the females' burrows.

Hungry Babies

The baby spiders must eat their way out of the egg sac when they are ready to hatch. Baby tarantulas look a lot like adults when they are first born. But they are tiny and have almost no color. They don't have claws or exoskeletons yet. The new spiders are quite hungry. Sometimes they eat one of their brothers or sisters!

Spiderlings usually leave their mother's burrow between three and six days after hatching. They have to be careful when they first leave the burrow. They would be a tasty treat for the many predators that like to eat tarantulas. The baby spiders dig homes for themselves and hide.

It takes about two to three years for most tarantulas to become fully grown. Some **species** take as long as nine years. Once they are grown, the tarantulas can have babies of their own.

Spiderlings begin eating live prey right after they are born.

CHAPTER 4

All in the Family

Tarantulas and other spiders have existed for millions of years. Many ancient species are now **extinct**. Scientists learn about these extinct animals from the fossils that they leave behind when they die. They can learn how long ago these animals walked Earth, how big they were, and how they survived.

Very few tarantula fossils have been discovered so far, but the ones that have been found tell us a lot. We know that tarantulas have changed very little over the past 20 million years or so. Tarantulas very similar to the ones we know today were alive at the same time as dinosaurs. The earliest known tarantula ancestors lived about 240 million years ago. Other spiders are even older. Scientists believe that some types of spiders may even have existed before dinosaurs.

Fossils are a valuable tool for learning about plant and animal species of the past.

Wolf Spiders

Tarantulas' closest relatives today come from the wolf spider family. Scientists group these spiders into two different families, but they are similar in many ways. Wolf spiders are fearsome predators. They got their name from the way they chase down prey like wolves do. They have sharp claws on their legs and strong jaws just as tarantulas do. They also live in burrows instead of building webs.

There are about 175 wolf spider species. None are quite as large as tarantulas. The largest species grows to a body length of about 1 inch (2.5 cm). Its legs are about the same length as its body.

FUN FACT! Some people in South America hunt Goliath bird-eating tarantulas for food.

Wolf spiders look a lot like small tarantulas.

Scorpions

Scorpions are another close relative of tarantulas. Unlike tarantulas, many scorpions are very dangerous to humans. They attack enemies using a stinger that is attached to the end of a long, curved tail. There are about 1,500 different scorpion species, and around 25 of them produce poison that is strong enough to kill people. Many others can cause severe pain and sickness. Experts estimate that hundreds of people die each year from scorpion stings.

Scorpions are found all around the world. Most of them live in desert **habitats**. Others make their homes in forests and grasslands.

People living in deserts must be careful to avoid the poisonous stings of scorpions.

The Tarantula's Tiny Cousin

The spruce-fir moss spider is one of the tarantula's smallest relatives. Spruce-fir moss spiders are much smaller than any tarantula species. They only grow to be about 0.2 inches (5 millimeters) long.

The spruce-fir moss spider is not a tarantula, but it shares many similarities with its larger cousin. Like tarantulas, it does not use a web to catch its food. It hides and waits for prey to pass by. It then uses its chelicerae to kill and eat the prey.

These tiny, rare spiders are only found in North Carolina and Tennessee. They live high up in mountainous areas where it gets very cold. Most spiders cannot live in such cold areas.

The spruce-fir moss spider is **endangered**. Very few of them are left in the wild. But scientists are working to save the species from extinction.

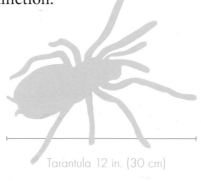

Tarantula 12 in. (30 cm)

Spruce-fir moss spider
.2 in. (5 mm)

The spruce-fir moss spider is very difficult to find in the wild.

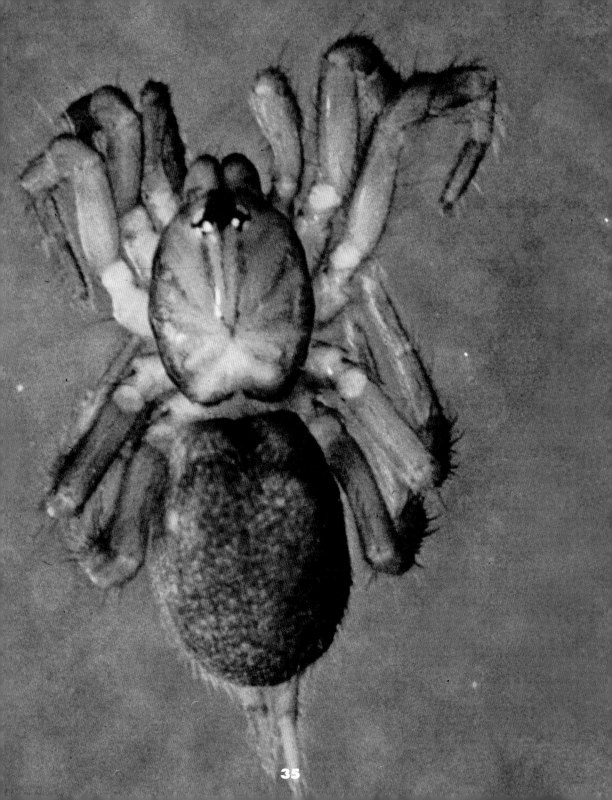

35

CHAPTER 5

The Future of Tarantulas

There are many different types of tarantulas. But scientists and environmentalists are worried that some species might disappear.
Some types of tarantulas are becoming rare because smugglers collect and sell them for pets. There are laws that limit how many tarantulas can be taken and what kinds can be sold. But some people break the rules to make money.

Tarantulas can make good pets. They're easy to care for. But they are not very cuddly. People must learn how to care for tarantulas before getting one as a pet. They must also make sure to buy tarantulas only from trustworthy sources.

Tarantulas need plenty of space to live and grow.

Vanishing Habitats

The human population has been growing incredibly quickly over the past several centuries. As it grows, people need more space and more resources. One way they get these things is by taking over the areas where tarantulas and other animals live. People cut down trees and other plants. They also drain water from wetter areas. This leaves less space for tarantulas to live. It also leaves less space for the animals that tarantulas rely on for food.

Some tarantulas are affected as logging companies cut down trees in forests. They use these trees to make wood and paper products.

Other tarantula habitats are destroyed so people can build bigger farms or new places to live. Habitat destruction is the biggest threat to many tarantula species today. Certain types of tarantulas might become extinct as they lose their homes.

Logging is a major threat to many of the world's rain forests.

Protecting Tarantulas

People around the world are working to make sure that these threats do not cause any tarantula species to become extinct. One way is to breed tarantulas away from their natural habitats. Tarantulas are collected from the wild and taken to zoos and other locations where they are safe. Scientists then allow the tarantulas to mate and produce young. The new tarantulas are later released back into the wild. It is much easier to do this for tarantulas than it is for many other endangered animals. This is because tarantulas are small enough that large numbers of them can live in just a single room at a zoo. Zoos in London, England, and Louisville, Kentucky, are among those helping to protect tarantula species.

Tarantulas are incredible animals. With a little help, they will continue to amaze us for many years to come.

Certain tarantula species make better pets than others.

Words to Know

barbed (BARBD) — a type of arrow, hook, or, in the case of the tarantula, hair that has sharp points that stick out

burrows (BUR-ohz) — tunnels or holes in the ground made or used as a home by a rabbit or other animal

cannibals (KAN-uh-buhlz) — animals that eat other animals of their own kind

carapace (KAHR-uh-pase) — the thick outer shell on the "head" of the tarantula

carnivores (KAR-nih-vorz) — animals that have meat as a regular part of their diet

cephalothorax (sef-uh-lo-THOR-aks) — the section of the tarantula that contains its brain, eyes, jaws, stomach, legs, and pedipalps

chelicerae (keh-LIH-suh-ree) — the tarantula's jaws

chitin (KIH-tin) — the hard material that makes up the exoskeleton of the tarantula

circulatory system (SIR-kyeh-leh-tor-ee SIS-tuhm) — the group of organs that pump blood through the body

egg sac (EGG SAK) — a special bag of spider silk that protects eggs until they hatch

endangered (en-DAYN-jurd) — at risk of becoming extinct, usually because of human activity

exoskeletons (ek-so-SKEH-luh-tunz) — hard outer coverings that protect and support an animal's internal organs and muscles

extinct (ik-STINGKT) — no longer found alive

glands (GLANDZ) — the part of the spider's body that produces silk

habitats (HAB-uh-tatz) — places where an animal or a plant is usually found invertebrates (in-VUR-tuh-brits) — animals without a backbone

mate (MAYT) — to join together to produce babies

molting (MOLT-ing) — shedding an old layer of feathers, skin, or an outer covering

paralyzes (PEHR-uh-ly-zez) — causes another animal to be unable to move

pedicle (PEH-dih-kuhl) — the narrow waist section between the abdomen and the cephalothorax

pedipalps (PEH-deh-palps) — small arms near the jaws that help the tarantula dig, move, and hold on to food

predators (PREH-duh-turz) — animals that live by hunting other animals for food

prey (PRAY) — an animal that's hunted by another animal for food

species (SPEE-sheez) — one of the groups into which animals and plants of the same genus are divided

spiderlings (SPY-dur-lingz) — newly hatched spiders

spinnerets (spin-uh-RETS) — tiny holes in the spider's abdomen where silk thread shoots out

trip lines (TRIP LINES) — silk threads that a tarantula uses to let it know food is nearby

valves (VALVZ) — parts of the body that have a flap that controls the flow of blood back to the tarantula's heart

venom (VEH-num) — poison produced by some snakes and spiders

vertebrates (VUR-tuh-brits) — animals that have a backbone

vibrations (vy-BRAY-shunz) — rapid motions back and forth; how a spider can tell that another creature is near

PACIFIC

OCEAN

NORTH

AMERICA

ATLANTI

SOUTH
AMERICA

Tarantula Range

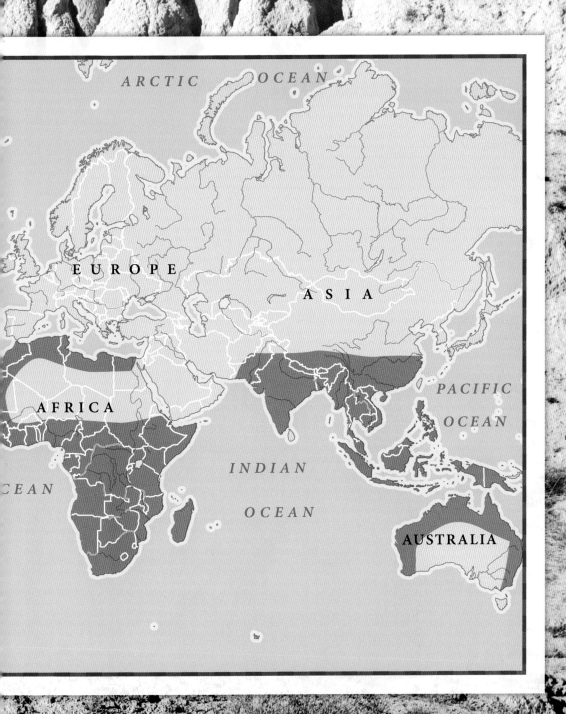

ARCTIC OCEAN

EUROPE

ASIA

AFRICA

PACIFIC OCEAN

INDIAN

OCEAN

OCEAN

AUSTRALIA

Find Out More

Books

Bishop, Nic. *Spiders*. New York: Scholastic Nonfiction, 2007.

Montgomery, Sy. *The Tarantula Scientist*. Boston: Houghton Mifflin Company, 2004.

Twist, Clint. *Tarantulas*. Milwaukee: Gareth Stevens Publishing, 2006.

Web Sites

Arizona-Sonora Desert Museum: Tarantula
www.desertmuseum.org/kids/oz/long-fact-sheets/tarantula.php
Find out more about tarantulas in the Arizona desert.

National Geographic: Tarantula
http://animals.nationalgeographic.com/animals/bugs/tarantula/
Learn some general information about tarantulas.

National Geographic Kids: Tarantulas
http://kids.nationalgeographic.com/kids/animals/creaturefeature/tarantulas/
Check out this video about the Goliath bird-eating tarantula.

Visit this Scholastic web site for more information on tarantulas:
www.factsfornow.scholastic.com

Index

About the Author

Vicky Franchino has written dozens of books for children, but this is her first book about spiders. She enjoyed learning more about creatures that many people think are "icky" (including one of her daughters!) and was excited to find out that spiders are actually very helpful creatures. She has never touched a tarantula, but she thinks it would be kind of fun! Vicky lives in Madison, Wisconsin, with her husband and daughters.
Photo by Kat Franchino